NLP

Discover How To Manipulate, Read People, And Exert Mental Control And Learn About The Strategies Of Influence And See How They Might Help You To Become Less Susceptible To Manipulation

(The Effective Method That Will Make Every Aspect Of Your Life Better)

WilfriedMarkovic

TABLE OF CONTENT

The Fundamental And Central Ideas Behind NLP 1

Why Is It Necessary For An Individual To Learn About Nlp? 7

Develop Your Communication Skills To The Next Level With Nlp 15

Conversion Of Behavior And Manipulation Of Behavior 24

Utilization Of Acquired Information 30

Goal Setting 39

Goal-Setting Using Nlp: Focusing On Well-Formed Outcomes 43

A Selection Of Methods For Mind Control 58

How Would You Describe The Optimal Setting For Thinking? 63

How To Control And Influence Your Own Nonverbal Communication 70

Hypnotic Methods And Techniques 76

When Does Telling Lies Turn Into Deception? 87

Accept The Responsibilities Associated 105

The Method Of Integrating Individual Parts. 109

A Few Different Domains In Which Neuro-Linguistic Programming, Also Known As Nlp, Can Be Of Service To You 116

Let's Get Started With The Anchoring 125

The Hypnotic State, Also Known As The Naturally Occurring Hypnotic State 129

How Neuro-Linguistic Programming (Nlp) Can Cure Ptsd More Efficiently Than Other Treatments Can. 131

The Psychology Of The Mentally Ill 137

What Exactly Is Meant By "Learning Capacity"?
.... 150

The Fundamental And Central Ideas Behind NLP

In the prior chapters, we spoke about the three different aspects that make up NLP. In this section, we will go further into the basic principles that influence NLP as well as the three components that make up NLP.

The presence of subjectivity

Anyone is capable of having subjective representations because of the experiences that they have had in their lives. Bandler and Grinder believe that the representation is composed of the five senses as well as the language that is used. The classical senses of hearing, smelling, tasting, and seeing are the components that make up the individual's subjective conscious experience. A excellent illustration of this would be when we have something "on our mind" and then think about what will happen based on "what we see," "what we hear," and "what we taste." The next step will be "what we smell," followed by "what we feel," and finally, it will easily lead to "what we think." The individual is affected as they establish a pattern and structure according to the subjective perceptions. At this point in time, NLP is thought of as the study that is utilised for any experience that is regarded to be subjective.

The sense-based and subjective representations of a person's life are the primary means by which their behaviour may be understood and described. It might be a non-verbal or vocal form of communication, it could be regarded incompetence, or it could be a pathological habit that affects any skilled practise in the same way. The manipulation or modification of the representations of the senses is capable of bringing about changes in the habits.

The experience of consciousness

This takes place when a person's thought, which was previously aware, subsequently transforms into one that has both conscious and unconscious components. The representations that occur on a person's consciousness are referred to as the unconscious mind, despite the fact that the representations themselves are subjective.

Acquiring Knowledge

Learning is accomplished via the process of modelling, which is more often known as imitation. It is well renowned for its capacity to assist in the production of experience in any endeavour. The knowledge of and ability to describe the description of the actions that are engaged is the most crucial aspect. And be aware of the process that was involved as well as the result.

The Foundational Elements of NLP

The Neuro-Linguistic Programming (NLP) framework is comprised of four well-known pillars or foundations, which are as follows:

The use of NLP makes it possible for everyone to form and keep positive relationships with the people in their environment. This is a promise. This is the capacity to get familiar with and establish a relationship with other individuals in a short amount of time. It will assist in the creation of trust with other individuals, and trust may be rapidly created when there is an understanding. By having knowledge of the desires of other people, their predictions, and having access to what their plans are.

Consciousness of the Sensations

Interacting with other people is the primary means via which this may be accomplished. Take, for example, the situation in which you are invited to the home of another individual. The first thing you are going to notice is their interior design, the aroma, the colours that are employed, and any sounds that are in the area. This is much different from the things that are found in your home. When you pay closer attention to the world around you and make full use of all of your senses, as neuro-linguistic programming (NLP) teaches you to do, you will find that everything seems to have a deeper level of meaning.

Thinking About the Results

When you set out to do anything, you should always have the end result, or aim, in mind. They assist in connecting what a person wants to achieve or what they would want to accomplish. This helps to prevent one from ruminating on any potentially unpleasant outcomes, and it is also extremely good for the mental and spiritual health of one. Taking this technique assists in determining which options and decisions are the most important and beneficial.

Behaviour that is pliable and adaptable in nature

This indicates that a person is capable of doing something differently from what they are used to doing in a comfortable manner. This occurs when the typical actions you take and the manner in which you carry them out are not responsive or realistic. Being adaptable is one of the most important skills you have while working with NLP clients. The use of NLP may assist in obtaining fresh viewpoints and also in developing behaviours that have a constructive effect.

Why Is It Necessary For An Individual To Learn About Nlp?

The advantages of using NLP as well as its applications have been discussed. Once again, please explain the need of your acquiring NLP knowledge. There are a variety of reasons, one of which is that one develops into an effective and excellent communicator.

• The ability to perceive non-verbal cues and communicate effectively grows with time.

• Heighten your sensitivity to your senses and your subconscious mind.

• Motivation is essential for empowerment.

• Get rid of your worries and anxieties.

• Capable of having a clear mind and keeping their emotions in check.

- Strive to become successful in both personal and professional friendships and relationships.

- There is an increase in both the success rate and the achievements.

- Get rid of your bad habits and work on being a more upbeat and optimistic person.

- The capability of successfully obtaining knowledge from other individuals.

- Be able to communicate in a timely and accurate manner.

The second thing I want to relate to you in terms of pacing and leading in relation to hypnotic rapport building is how that pacing is almost like following that person in some capacity; that is to say, pacing their pace and movement and direction in terms of where they are at with it. In other words, I want to tell you how that pacing is almost like following that individual in some capacity. You are giving that individual permission to be who they really are in the most natural condition that they now find themselves in. Next, you will begin to assert some control over the situation by convincing the other person to accept you. You will do this by simply providing them with an idea or reasoning that is comprehensible to them. Then you are leading them by changing directions and having them follow you into a new point of reference, and you are doing this by leading them. Pacing and leading in sales is mostly accomplished via the use of yessets. If you are not acquainted with the concept, using a yes set, you are effectively repeating back to the consumer what they stated they wanted and tagging on a question asking if they are correct or whether they are wrong in making that statement. Making it in the form of a question requires the prospective buyer to either agree with what you are saying or acknowledge that you are correct. You go about for a while, all the time having that other person agree with you, and then you say something that they did not initially say, but which is merely probable, which in this circumstance is a leading statement, and you see whether they agree with you or not. Your pacing and leading pattern has effectively won you the required rapport if they agree with you; this makes it feasible for them to agree with you without feeling the need to resist agreeing with you and eliminates the need for them to feel the need to resist agreeing with you.

The final item I want you to consider in relation to pacing and leading is the conversational element of pacing and leading when it comes to communicating with others. You really need to be aware of the fact that you'll be engaging in a substantial amount of conversation if you plan on working in sales. But you presumably already knew that, considering how clear it is to you. When you are having a discussion with a possible client, one thing you can do to control the flow of the conversation is to regulate the pace at which someone is speaking. This can be done by either slowing down or speeding up the person who is speaking. For instance, you may calibrate to a person's tone, pitch, volume, and tempo in order to pace their natural speaking pace. After doing so, you can abruptly begin to slow down the discussion, speed it up according to your needs, alter the tone, etc. in order to pace the person's natural speaking pace. It's possible that you're wondering, "What does it mean to have such a strong hold on the conversation?" The relevance will be determined by the circumstances around it. When you are in a scenario in which you do not have a lot of time to chat, it may be helpful to speed up the discussion in order to get you to the point where you need to be. Another situation may be one in which the person is speaking so quickly that they are able to dominate the discussion and do not give you the opportunity to get a word in edgewise. Therefore, in this specific setting, slowing down the discussion may have the benefit of allowing you to take charge and steer the topic in the direction that you wanted it to go.

When we get into representational systems later on, you will learn about how individuals process information, and you will discover that most people process information mostly via one specific representational system, such as their visual, auditory, kinesthetic, olfactory, or gustatory representational system. And the dominant representational resource that is mostly represented will typically influence how quickly or slowly a person normally talks. This is because dominant representational resources are largely represented. For instance, a visual person has a greater propensity to talk more quickly than a kinesthetic person does. People who are more auditory tend to talk more clearly and in a tone that is somewhere in the center of what people who are more visual and people who are more kinesthetic say. An auditory person may have the tendency to speak more slowly to a visual person and repeat what they just said to them in a clearer manner so that the auditory person may better comprehend the visual person. others who are more auditory are more likely to be bothered by background noise, whereas others who are more visually oriented are less likely to be bothered by it.

Develop Your Communication Skills To The Next Level With Nlp

Anyone who has a strong interest in the subjects of communication and persuasion and wants to enhance his or her ability to convince others should look into neuro-linguistic programming, often known as NLP. This is one of the most effective applied psychology systems available. If you are aware of the specific ways in which people interact, you will be able to perceive the true matrix of communication. This applies whether individuals communicate face-to-face, over the phone, or by any other technological means such as email, texting, or online chatting.

Exchange of information

Relationship building

When two people are able to synchronize their brainwaves to the same frequencies, they are able to develop rapport with one another. This means that they are able to clearly comprehend and sympathize with what the other person is saying or where he is coming from. When both parties are in this condition, communication between them becomes much more strong and natural as a result of the mutual trust that exists between them.

In order to achieve this empathetic condition, neuro-linguistic practitioners often follow the following pattern:

a reflection of

Refers to being aware of the other party's behaviors and gestures, as well as the significant words (trance words) and personal values that they are communicating, which you will then attempt to feed back to the original speaker. People have faith in themselves, and the more they see you as a mirror of who they are, the more likely it is that they will believe what you say.

Please take note that mirroring does not imply that one is engaging in plagiarism. It must be subtle, to the point that it is virtually undetectable, yet nevertheless apparent to the unconscious mind of the individual.

The Art of Leading and Pacing

You may show that you have an appreciation for the other person's reality by pointing out things that are irrefutable in his present circumstance. This is what is meant by the term "pacing," which implies that you are displaying that you have a respect for the other person's reality.

Taking someone else by the hand and guiding them in the direction you want them to go is an example of leadership.

The typical sequence goes like this: Pace, Pace, Pace, and Lead. Which ultimately evolves into Pace, Pace, Lead, Lead.Pace, Pace, Lead. After some time, the pattern changes to Pace, Lead, Lead, Lead.

Let's imagine you're a guy who's interested in striking up a conversation with a stunning woman you encounter in the shopping center; how can we put this idea into practice?

You probably will think it's odd since we don't know one other and everything, but hello, may I please have your name? I know it's absolutely random, and you probably will think it's weird too, but hello!

When you have established a good connection with someone, you will need to make fewer pace remarks and will be able to get away with more leading. A good illustration of this might be, "Oh, you are just waiting for a friend (P), right?" Very nice! Let's go take a seat over there (L), and while we're there, you can tell me more about yourself (L). On the other hand, you should text your buddy to let her know where you are (L).

That is only an example, and the same strategy may be used for a variety of other purposes as well, such as resolving issues in the family, negotiating a lower price on a vehicle, etc.

Achieving the highest possible levels of health

You have undoubtedly realized by now that the Powerspin technique may be used for the creation of a wide variety of very uplifting states of mind.

When coping with health difficulties, the "rose-colored glasses" effect may be achieved by remembering and experiencing the following states, assigning each feeling a color, and then doing a Powerspin as in the previous example. Then consider life, particularly your current condition of health, as if it were tinted with that color.

(a) The sensation of being healthy. Think back to a moment when you felt particularly well and healthy, or try to envision a time in the future when you will feel incredibly well and healthy. Become familiar with the EMOTIONS that come from being in that experience. Give the FEELINGS some kind of shade.

(b) A sensation of excitement. Think back to a moment when you had an overwhelming sense of excitement. Achieve that state of enthusiasm right now, and then assign a color to this FEELING.

(c) The emotion of acceptance. Think back to a moment when someone made you feel that they welcomed you without any limitations, and you accepted them in the same way. The process is often less difficult with younger children and infants. In the event that this is not possible, you could find that having a pet, such as a dog, cat, or rabbit, can help you to relive that experience in your imagination and get the SENSE of mutual acceptance. Give the SENSE of what you're feeling a color.

(d) The emotion of love. Find a time in your life when you felt love for someone or something to its fullest extent and reflect on it. Give the emotion a colorwhile you mentally recreate the event you just had in your head.

(e) Have faith in your feelings. Think back to a time when you put your faith in another person and you were rewarded for doing so. You are aware that your decision to trust them was correct. One such illustration of this would be taking a trip on a train. You put your faith in the conduct of the driver, the signalman, and the track itself to guarantee that you arrive at your destination without incident, and it turned out that your faith was well-placed. Get that sense of trust, and then give that sense of trust a color.

(f) The state of being happy. Try to recall a time in the past when you were filled with joy and write it down. The arrival of a new baby, the realization of a goal, or the participation in any other fantastic event all contributed to the joyous emotions. Imagine that you are in the scene, reliving the event, and experiencing those positive emotions to the fullest extent that you are able to. Create an accompanying image (remember that stuff??). Give that joyful emotion a hue of its own.

Make the disc with the six sections, and then one at a time, place each of the different colors into the appropriate section of the disc. If you want the colors to blend together, look through the tube while you spin the disc, beginning off slowly and working your way up to full speed.

Imagine you are wearing the glasses of the color that is created when the colors are spun, and try to picture what it would be like to look at health problems through those lenses.

Some of our students have actually been successful in locating eyeglasses or sunglasses that have lenses of the color that they have designed, and they have reported having a good time while doing so.

There are some individuals who believe that there is some aspect of their life in which they need greater self-assurance. If you were to ask them to define confidence, the responses you would get would include a range of feelings.

When you put yourself through certain emotional states on Powerspin, you may sometimes very rapidly get a feeling of self-assurance. The most confident you can be is when

Conversion Of Behavior And Manipulation Of Behavior

Everything that you need to know about manipulation and mind control will be covered in the chapter that comes after this one. Do you want to guarantee that you can convince other people to appreciate the same things that you do? Are you interested in enhancing your lifestyle, convincing other individuals to get anything, and accomplishing a great deal more? If this is the case, then you are going to love this manual, particularly if you are interested in learning about manipulation and the ways in which it may benefit you.

What Exactly Is Manipulation?

When it comes to manipulation, it appears that many people grossly underestimate how strong it can be, and often, they will misinterpret what is going on with this art form as a result of this misconception. When people hear the term "manipulation," they often immediately jump to the conclusion that the other person is attempting to be emotionally abusive, nasty, or cruel. This is a widespread misconception. When we hear certain words, a large number of unfavorable connotations immediately come to mind.

It is vital to keep in mind that while some individuals may use manipulation in a bad way, there are also some beneficial aspects of manipulation that should not be forgotten. Because so many people have a bad view of manipulation, it may be difficult for them to understand how effective of a psychological art form manipulation can be. In addition, a lot of people don't realize that pretty much all of us are already manipulating others in one way or another just by going about our day-to-day lives, but they fail to realize this fact. Even if we don't immediately recognize this sort of conduct as manipulative, most of us have had some experience working with it in one form or another.

Learning how to successfully manipulate does not imply you are going to go out into the world and attempt to develop some abusive patterns between yourself and the people around you. Instead, it just indicates that you are aware of what it is that you want and have made improvements to the strategy that you plan to use in order to achieve your goal. If someone does not want to give in to what it is that you want, they will not give in to what it is that you want in the end.

The act of exerting pressure on another individual is just one component of manipulation. The most skilled manipulators are those who know not to coerce others into doing anything they don't voluntarily wish to do. Rather, it is more about making someone see the benefit in assisting you and doing what you would want them to do, and then expanding from there. Before we start to look at some of the strategies that you may use with manipulation, we first need to go further into what manipulation is all about, how and why manipulation tends to work, and when you would decide to work with manipulation in your own life.

It may be difficult for those who do not have a comprehensive understanding of manipulation and what it entails to recognize that this process is comprised of three stages. The vast majority of us will conceive of manipulation as a single act; nevertheless, there are two other things that must occur in addition to the act of manipulation in order to guarantee that the manipulation will be effective. These include the analysis, which comes first, and the persuading, which is going to take place throughout the most of the discussion with the victim, but is largely going to show up after the manipulation has taken place. Both of these come after the manipulation. If you realize that there is more to the art of manipulation than simply the act of manipulation itself, you will be able to have a better understanding of the factors that might contribute to the process's level of success. You will soon discover that the outcomes aren't as good if you omit these two elements, and that you are less likely to acquire the things that you desire, even if novices may believe that they can do it without the persuasion and the analytical portions of it. However, beginners may think that they can do it without these features since they are less experienced.

Utilization Of Acquired Information

The modeling process begins with a number of essential assumptions. The first is that the sensory systems that we utilize to depict our realities are responsible for processing the experience that we have. In other words, the job of janitor is awful in the eyes of one particular individual. One person's miserable life might be another person's paradise. One person's idea of a satisfying life is having money and a solid profession, whereas another person's idea of a meaningful life is having money and a steady career in addition to other activities that please them. The modeling process starts with the assumption that humans take in information about their surroundings via their senses and then process and remember that data. When this data is stored, it gives rise to memories, which are subsequently associated with visuals, auditory cues, olfactory cues, tactile sensations, and the like.

Unconscious mental representations make up a significant portion of this total. Take, for example, any one of your regular activities. Whether you are making coffee, tying your shoes, driving to work, brushing your teeth, or moving about your place of residence, your brain is accessing memories that enable you to act in the appropriate manner.

When we mimic a "template" in NLP, we are basically adopting the behaviors, language, techniques, and beliefs of that exemplar in order to duplicate the behavioral result of success. This is done in order to model the "template's" behavioral outcome. Of course, modeling is not limited to the conventional definition of "success," which refers to one's ability to run a firm and make money. It also has the potential to influence a wide variety of human learning. In the end, the newly acquired perspectives, cognitive patterns, emotional reactions, and behavioral consequences provide solutions to a wide range of problems and challenges.

Fears and phobias, mood disorders such as depression, habit disorders such as obsession and compulsion, psychosomatic diseases (thinking you are unwell when you are not), physical maladies, and learning disabilities are examples of the types of issues that fall into this category.

To put it another way, if we appropriately apply NLP to our lives, it has the power to completely transform everything about them. The power of efficient programming cannot be denied, whether it is in a professional or personal setting.

NLP can improve one's understanding of their thoughts, emotions, and behaviors; it can increase and maintain motivation; it can streamline values related to money, career, health, relationships, and family; it can attract compatible people; it can reduce and eliminate maladaptive thoughts and choices; it can discharge maladaptive elements from one's past; it can identify outcomes and goals; it can proactively approach goals; it can maintain quality relationships; and it can reduce or apply damaging stress.

* Achieve your highest possible level of physical and mental health * Construct a positive image of yourself * * * * Establish an Almost Instantaneous Rapport

NLP can help you achieve success in your job or career by doing the following: * Setting and achieving goals * Reducing barriers * Eliminating unwanted behaviors * Fostering strong and lasting partnerships * Minimizing cultural and contextual limitations * Facilitating communication * Supercharging negotiation skills * Maximizing conflict resolution * Improving sales * Improving workplace synergy * Boosting productivity

This method of working on practices and narrowing them down to simply their essential facets is analogous to the approach that is used in business processes, which aim to outline a series of actions and determine which ones are essential and which ones are not. In this view, the most typical method of improving procedures by making use of NLP should be made apparent for the aim of ensuring that individuals are efficient.

NLP is also concerned with the problem of determining the differences between two groups of people operating in the same environment: those who are successful and those who are not. The goal of success modeling is to determine, in contrast to someone who was unsuccessful in the same area of life, precisely what it was that successful individuals did to achieve their achievements. Have they considered the matter in a manner that was not expected? Were they surprised by the alternatives that were available to them? Were there any tendencies or behaviors on their part that helped to have an influence on the outcomes they got?

As a result, the fundamental perspective of NLP may be summed up as identifying and enhancing the factors that contribute to the outcome of a certain scenario in the form of an interaction model. When this model has been identified and refined, it very well may be employed to get radical results in a short amount of time. This might happen once it has been completed. This is due to the fact that the extensive amounts of time and effort that have led to successful people carrying out activities in a certain manner may be quickly and readily adopted by anybody who is ready to do so.

This deeper understanding of NLP is necessary for attaining Dark NLP, yet it is just half of the dilemma. Understanding the mundane mental norms that the typical NLP approach to looking at human behavior is filtered through is also very important. This is because these are the criteria that are used to determine what constitutes acceptable behavior. This innovative paradigm has the potential to combine the unfiltered truth of boring mental information with the manipulative productivity of NLP to produce a really unique model of comprehension. Which therefore brings us to the question: what are the key dim mental notions that have an affect on NLP?

One of the major ideas that sheds light on Dark NLP is the concept that individuals lack significant personality traits and are, as a result, unable to resist the influence of others, whether that influence is for the better or for the worst. Traditional NLP acknowledges this understanding of lifestyle as being fluid and makes use of it as a purpose for professionals to support people in overcoming the substantial hurdles that are holding them back during their daily existence. According to another interpretation of Dark NLP, this smoothness of personality denotes that an individual is capable of being led into doing as suggested by the desire of other people. The fact that some individuals are able to succumb to the allure of shadowy influences like extremist ideologies or cults is proof of the existence of this potential for malevolent influence.

In addition, research on the dark side of the brain has shown that individuals have less control over their own free will than they commonly believe they have. When questioned, the vast majority of people would say that they are generally in command of their own views, and they will also state that they wouldn't submit to a guideline that is in direct opposition to their own fundamental autonomy if it were presented to them. This misconception is cleared up by a well-known experiment in the field of brain research, which had a direct influence on the concepts that dark brain science proposes. Volunteers in the famous Milgram experiment were instructed to administer electric shocks to themselves if they provided a response that was off base during a learning exam. Even though they were supposedly able to hear the individual being punished screaming, the vast majority of those who were ordered to deliver the shocks proceeded to do so. This trial demonstrates that people have a natural deference to authority and less freedom of choice than they would very typically anticipate, both of which are innate characteristics. In a similar vein, the well-known Zimbardo study provides insight into an additional viewpoint that bolsters the field of dark brain research. This viewpoint is the willingness of humans to anticipate behaviors based on the role they play in some random event. According to

Zimbardo's interpretation, the participants were arbitrarily classified as either prison watchmen or detainees. As the test progressed, the candidates who were selected for the role of prison monitor showed an increasing willingness to carry out acts of cruelty and excessive use of force.

Goal Setting

Setting goals is an essential part of any kind of NLP. You will be able to create objectives that are both achievable and exciting after you have determined what it is that you really want out of life and from NLP. Now is the time for you to consider the objectives you have set. If you don't already have any fascinating and exciting objectives that get your heart pumping, it's time to set some new ones.

After that, you should put out your objectives. You may even engage in a fun activity, such as constructing a goal board. You may get a craft board and then adorn it with photos and sketches of the things you want to achieve. Position your goal list or board in a place where it will be easy for you to notice it. This will help you to maintain your objectives at the forefront of your mind and motivate you to work toward them on a daily basis. Having a written record of your objectives might help you improve your visualization skills, which is a fundamental aspect of NLP.

Having a Higher Level of Energy

Having more energy is almost always a desirable trait. To make progress toward your objectives, you will certainly need to have it. Caffeine and sugary energy drinks may provide you with a temporary boost of energy, but the chemical energy spikes they cause often result in a severe collapse later on. It is preferable to gain one's energy in a method that is natural and not harmful. Without the use of any form of pharmacological stimulant, you may increase your energy levels just by changing your mental state on your own.

The key to having boundless amounts of energy is to pursue interests that really excite you. You can do anything if you follow your passion. You are going to be overcome with an incredible amount of energy. Either cultivate a deep-seated desire for the accomplishment of your objectives, or look for brand-new obstacles to overcome. Your lack of energy is likely due to the fact that you do not feel motivated.

Imagine if each day is a huge orange as soon as you open your eyes in the morning. This orange has been patiently waiting for you to peel it so that you may savor the juicy pulp in the middle. If you are starving, you won't give it a second thought before you start peeling that orange. In all honesty, it is not that difficult of a task. Imagine that the activities you have to do during the day are likewise enormous oranges that are simply waiting to be peeled and devoured. Approach each and every activity as if it were not a burden but rather one of the necessary stepping stones on the path to achievement.

Goal-Setting Using Nlp: Focusing On Well-Formed Outcomes

One of the high-level NLP concepts that has practical application in the working world is the notion of well-formed outcomes. It's a method for defining objectives that gives them a sense of being grounded in reality and within reach. It makes SMART Goals appear like a child's toy when it comes to being a technique!

It is a vital management talent to be able to guide someone toward a goal that is not only personally appealing to them but also beneficial to them in the long run.

The inquiry "What do you want?" is the first thing that is asked.

Be careful you phrase it in a way that others will desire it, rather than as something they don't want. But if they have trouble articulating it, you may try to pry out of them what it is that they do not want and then urge them to investigate what viable alternatives there are. What are you doing, feeling, or having that you don't want to be doing, feeling, or having? is a nice question to start with in order to get you thinking about this.

After that, you may inquire, "what would you prefer instead?"

Next, find out what their 'evidence method' is by asking, "How will you know when you've got it?"

This assures that the objective is something they will be able to check and feel good about, in addition to giving the impression that the goal is more genuine to them. Additionally, it assumes that they will be successful. In contrast, the question "how would you know if you got it?" is far less persuasive.

A question such as "What will you see, hear, and feel, when you've got it?" is one way to make the evidence process more explicit.

You will be able to extract more intense sensory language from them in their description of the outcome, which will result in it having a greater impact on them.

Now, check to see if the objective is framed inside a rational framework by asking, "When and where do you want it?"

Insist on receiving responses that are as precise as is humanly feasible. In addition to what is frequently referred to as a "ecology check," you may supplement it with inquiries such as "For what purpose do you want this?"

Now it's time to provide them the incentive they need to start working toward the objective. Inquire with the question, "What will you get when you've got it?"

Other possible variations include the question, "What do you stand to gain or lose once you have it?"

"What will have transpired by the time you have obtained it?

If you want to increase their drive even further, you might also ask them, "What will happen if you don't act to get it?" This is a question that is sure to get them thinking.

It is now time to assist them in considering available resources.

"What resources do you have at your disposal to assist you in achieving this result?"

These may take the form of monetary or material resources, as well as individuals who may provide assistance or support. After saying this, you may follow up by asking, "What other resources might you require?"

And then you may augment this by asking, "Who can assist you in acquiring those resources?"

Where are you able to get such resources for your own use?

Last but not least, you should encourage them to get moving by asking them something along the lines of, "What are you going to do to begin now to get what you want?"

It's possible that you'll need to assist them with anything along the lines of, "What is the first step you are going to take?"

A well-formed result must always be those things at all times:

In all likelihood capable of accomplishment

Put into motion by the proprietor

Maintained by the owner until such time as they either realize their goal or determine that pursuing it is no longer the best course of action for them

Beneficial for the owner

Presented in a good manner

Reactions from the Senses

We will now go on to the next issue, which is the activation of our sensory responses from when we were children. You probably learnt about the five senses that are responsible for sending messages to the brain while you were in elementary school. These five senses—sight, hearing, touch, smell, and taste—are considered to be so fundamental to human existence that we refer to them as the "five essential senses." NLP, in general, makes use of these five senses in a constructive manner to boost both performance and overall levels of energy:

1. Visual communication is made possible through the eyes.

2. Communication via sound is made possible through the hearing.

3. The sense of touch is facilitated by the skin.

4. The ability to smell is provided by the nose.

5. The ability to taste comes from the mouth, the tongue, and the taste buds.

Because these five senses will play a significant role in future sessions, it is essential that you commit them to memory as one of the core ideas underlying NLP. These five senses are going to be the tools that we utilize to bring more optimism into our lives.

The following essay will devote some attention to each of these five senses. I will provide some peeks into several methods that I have received training in. For instance, we desire the reactions and activation of the senses in order to check in with our friends, and we need to have experiences and the sensation of executing each response on a consistent basis. There is also the option of recalling our younger years. You will be given various photographs to serve as prompts, and for each picture, you will be required to identify five or six distinct sensory signals.

Rule no. 4: The mind and the body are mutually influential.

The mind and the body are related since they are both parts of the same integrated and complicated system, and as a result, they have an effect on one another. It is impossible to have a mind that is distinct from your body. When taken apart, these two terms have very little significance since they operate as if they were a single entity and have a mutually reinforcing effect on one another. Even if you are only visualizing it, when you think about biting into a slice of pizza, your mind reacts as if you have already eaten even though you are just thinking about it.

Rule number five: Provide a diverse selection of behaviors or options. Take Command of the System

When it comes to human systems, control refers to the capacity to exercise influence on one's experiences both at the moment they occur and over the course of time. You will have a greater degree of control over the situation if you are able to exhibit a greater degree of behavioral flexibility, that is, if you have a greater number of different ways of behaving, interacting, and thinking. It is always better to have a choice rather than to have none at all. There is no exception to this rule. In this regard, the greater the number of options available to you, the better. This idea is strongly connected to the third rule, which discusses changing one's conduct until one has achieved their objectives. If what you are doing is not producing the desired results, then why not adjust your actions and try something else until you discover something that does provide the desired results? You should not give up on anything just because it did not work out the first time; failure is a natural part of life and should not discourage you from trying again.

The sixth and final rule: adaptation and conduct

The path to adaptation is ultimately determined by how you act. Your first adaptation is going to be determined by the environment from which that behavior originates. Your reality is often defined by what you recognize and consider to be true about the outside world. Your actions demonstrate how well you have adjusted to the world that you have constructed for yourself. Your actions, regardless of how well they work, are a reflection of how well you have adapted to the environment at a certain point in time. On the other hand, it's possible that your response to a certain circumstance won't be appropriate in another one. For instance, context may be characterized as the circumstance in which you are confronted by a bear at a zoo and another situation in which the bear is hot on your trail when you are in the wilderness. The key to understanding the difference between these two scenarios is how you react to each one.

The idea behind social proof is that... This principle may seem strange and out of the ordinary, but in reality, it is not at all like that at all. It's a rather straightforward occurrence that we see occurring all around us on a daily basis. This idea relies on the straightforward concept of individuals who are prepared to undertake something that a large number of other people have previously done. The concept of social proof is quite similar to that of social influence.

It may come as a surprise to learn that the majority of marketers rely on this concept as the primary marketing strategy to convince and influence their potential clients to make a purchase of their goods. When promoting a product, you've probably heard businesses make the claim that hundreds of individuals are already utilizing their product and are happy with the outcomes of doing so. There is a justification for the assertion made by the company that hundreds of people are currently utilizing their product. The rationale for this is so that people are aware that they aren't the only one using it, and that there are many other people utilizing it; this naturally transmits the notion that the product is useful. When a potential customer sees this, all they think about is the fact that other people have also used the product, leading them to reason that it must be a good one since at the very least they are willing to give it a go.

Therefore, when you are attempting to convince someone of anything, it is best to come up with some kind of social evidence that you can share with others. You may do this by stating something along the lines of, "All of my customers use this product, and they are so pleased with its results that they keep coming back for more."

There are industry experts that I have come across who have made excellent use of this approach in order to increase the number of customers who purchase their goods or engage them for their services. These individuals had launched their endeavor by providing their services pro bono and putting in their utmost effort in doing so. It was instantly considered a social proof if one of their customers remarked how much they enjoyed dealing with them. The expert might easily encourage their potential client to cooperate with them by referring to their previous experiences collaborating with other customers by citing such experiences.

It takes talent to be able to convince someone of anything, but it's more of an accomplishment to amass enough social evidence to make your own convincing an easy stroll in the park!

A Selection Of Methods For Mind Control

The position of a leader is not an easy one to do. Controlling people is one of the most time-consuming and tough tasks that leaders need to do at work, despite the fact that it is also one of the most important tasks.

In this chapter, we will examine a few different mind-controlling tactics that will make it much simpler for a leader to exert authority over a group of followers.

a system of rewards and punishments

The reward and punishment system is the first sort of strategy that may be used for mind control. By putting into action the method, not only will you have a simple time comprehending it but you will also have complete command over all of your workers.

It requires you to make an announcement to your staff that

whomever has the greatest performance will be rewarded, and whoever has the lowest performance will be disciplined.

This is a simple method, yet it yields excellent results. The workers are going to compete with one another in a spirit of healthy healthy competitiveness.

You need to maintain a close check on your personnel and choose the most qualified candidates. You are also need to identify and catalog the personnel with the lowest levels of productivity.

You will have to show favoritism to the first few and be harsh with the remaining few. Keep in mind that the award ought to be something that is really valuable as well as something that the workers will enjoy.

On the other hand, the severity of the penalty ought not to be excessive. It need to be something like remaining behind at work for a half an hour longer than usual after each shift, or some other similar kind of punishment.

You are required to make an effort to choose a distinct winner and also a new individual to penalize each time. It's possible that an employee may feel pressured and awful if they are both praised and reprimanded for the same behavior.

Keep in mind that you should not let them know your objectives of attempting to exert any kind of control over them by disclosing these methods. They have to believe that you are acting in the company's best interest by doing so.

Some individuals employ a novel strategy in which they provide positive reinforcement for a certain behavior one week, and then turn around and offer negative reinforcement for same behavior the following week. In most cases, this is done to discourage individuals from engaging in the same pattern of behavior over an extended period of time. They will be able to exert influence over the ideas and behaviors of the various people by cultivating an atmosphere that is fraught with uncertainty.

You may use a tactic quite similar to this one to exert authority over your family members or over your children at home. You have the responsibility of announcing awards for all of those who are doing their part at home, while also announcing punishments for those who are not performing their task correctly. For instance, you could commend them if they keep their room clean on a regular basis and also do a good job of keeping the home, but you should reprimand them if they throw trash on the ground.

After they have been disciplined, they will reflect on what they did wrong and be less likely to do it again. You may also choose to penalize your children if they do not complete their assigned homework and choose to praise them if they complete their assignments in an accurate manner.

Therefore, this method of rewarding and punishing will be effective in all contexts. You may use it in any situation in which you need to exert authority over other people.

Procedure based on reactions

The next method is called the response method, and it's the one after that. It is one in which you give the worker compliments in order to get the very best performance out of them. The reaction approach is every bit as efficient as the one that came before it. It is one in which you will have the opportunity to have a favorable effect on the other person. A system of rewards and/or punishments is not required in order to accomplish this goal. Simply letting them know that you have a lot of trust in them and that you think they are the finest employee in the organization is all that is required of you at this point. This will inspire them to perform to the best of their abilities.

These are the two approaches of mind control that you may use to exert authority over the thoughts of your employees.

How Would You Describe The Optimal Setting For Thinking?

You don't have to be a thinker to achieve this, but you do need to figure out what type of atmosphere you thrive in. Which would you rather have—complete quiet or a little bit of noise? When do you find that you are most creative? While some individuals are wide awake and aware in the morning, others find that their productivity is most in the evening.

It is not always feasible to ponder when in the atmosphere that is most beneficial to you. Because of this, it is quite vital to be familiar with your own style and to have the ability to adapt to different environments. People who are naturally active at night may find it more appealing to work from home at night so that they are not have to go to work each day. Depending on the company they work for, a night owl can try to negotiate working from home on an off-shift. Technology has made it feasible to work remotely in a wide variety of occupations.

People who demand complete isolation in order to think effectively have several choices available to them because to technological advancements. Think about asking your manager if you might work somewhere other than the main office, such as a conference room or a more peaceful corner of the building. Because of the proliferation of portable electronic devices such as mobile phones and laptop computers, almost any area may now function as a workstation.

It might be challenging for you to get up and leave your office or desk setting. Consider, as an alternative, the ways in which you might tailor your working environment to better accommodate the way you think. It is possible for you to silence the ringing on your desk phone, and you should schedule a little amount of time daily to check and reply to your messages. This is assuming that you do not have any pressing issues that need your attention. If you live in a cubicle, you should politely urge your neighbors to keep the noise level down. Open floor layouts are not the best choice for this purpose. You always have the option to work on significant assignments in a setting that is more suitable to your job, such as the night owl thinker.

People who are able to function normally despite the presence of some background noise are more adaptive than those who do not need it. They are able to function well despite the ambient disturbances that are present in typical working situations and may create a tranquil space for oneself by listening to music or putting the television on at a low volume to simulate white noise. Some individuals believe that too much stimulation is uninteresting, while others find that being in an environment with a lot of noise makes them feel more connected to others and gives them more energy.

It's possible that some people may discover that engaging in other hobbies might really improve their thinking. There have been a lot of instances in which a lightbulb in the shower has suddenly turned off. Sometimes, in order for our brains to do their mental acrobatics, they require our attention to be focused on physical action. The amount of blood and oxygen that reaches the brain may be increased by running or going for a run. It is a fantastic method to get your mind going and assist you in finding solutions to difficulties.

What exactly is the relationship between all of this and NLP? The foundation of neuro-linguistic programming is your unique way of thinking. Before beginning to practice NLP, it is essential to have a solid understanding of your own thoughts. If you are able to identify the sort of thinker you are and utilize this information as a jumping off point for your NLP experience, you will find that it is both more gratifying and successful. You may now pose the following questions to yourself:

Are you more of a linear thinker or an abstract thinker?

Is it an emotional response or a stoic one?

How can I make better use of my imagination, or what are some ways that I might improve it?

Which of these three stances best describes your outlook on life?

Where are I most productive in my thinking?

What kind of atmosphere, stimulation, or activities are most conducive to my most productive thinking?

- What is the general makeup of my thinking profile? We'll go on to discussing how you can apply yourself and utilize NLP to shape and modify your ideas via mind management and compartmentalization now that you have a good idea of the sort of thinker you are. This is a significant step in neuro-linguistic programming, and you will utilize the information you get from it in all of your future NLP endeavors. Let's take another look at it, shall we?

CONTROL OF ONE'S MIND

Have you ever had a feeling that your thoughts were so disorganized that you were unable to select what action to do next? You could have read the same paragraph many than once, or you might not have been able to focus on what you were reading for a long enough period of time for you to comprehend it. You may have also driven yourself nuts attempting to accomplish a job that you have finished thirty minutes ago. It is possible to have feelings of being overwhelmed as well as an inability to focus. Using some fundamental NLP techniques for managing your thoughts, you can get your life back on track.

How To Control And Influence Your Own Nonverbal Communication

The consensus amongst authorities is that you can teach yourself to regulate it by being aware of your own body language and that you can even actively employ it to make communication far simpler.

It is highly recommended that you create videos and watch them without the audio playing. Before beginning a session, try calming yourself down with some breathing and mindfulness techniques so that you can be more aware of how your body is moving.

It may also be helpful to adjust your body language in a manner that is purposeful in order to improve your communication with another individual. This technique, which is known as mirroring, demands that you comprehend and then discreetly imitate the facial movements, body posture, tone of voice, and other micro-expressions that are being sent by the individual with whom you are conversing. To some, this may seem to be deceptive or false; nonetheless, I think that imitating that type of synchronicity clearly makes it possible for you to convey your genuine feelings more correctly and prevents others from misinterpreting what you are trying to say.

However, use caution. Expert and author Janine Driver, who has spent the past decade training federal agents how to interpret the body language of suspects during investigations, cautions that attempting to control your body language may end up backfiring if it is not done effectively. Driver has spent the last decade teaching federal agents how to perceive the body language of suspects during investigations. If you fixate on a single piece of information without considering how it fits into the whole picture, you run the danger of making a mistake that might have serious consequences.

"Trying to use body language by reading a dictionary on body language is similar to learning to talk French by reading a dictionary in French. Neither approach will get you very far." Your actions look to be fabricated, and your talents in body language appear to be disconnected from one another. I would recommend that you endeavor to refine and articulate your natural body language rather than attempting to change or mask it. In this way, your body language will complement rather than detract from the message that you are intending to portray.

Physically touching the person you are speaking with might be helpful.

Unable to see the forest for the trees (shortsightedness, insecurity).

Slouchy bodily position (caused by boredom and being alone).

Assume an erect and protective stance with your body.

Smiling, lean forward (friendly, if not excessive).

The language of the body, which includes hand and arm gestures, body posture and motions, facial gestures and eye movements, and other types of body language, may reveal what we think about other people, most of the time without our conscious awareness.

Cognitive psychologists assert that the human species evolved a significant amount of time before spoken human language, the capability to interpret implicit physical signs, and the ability to form opinions about a person based on specific signals.

Body language, much like spoken language, tends to shift significantly from one civilization to the next. It's possible that different nations have significantly different interpretations of the same gesture.

The body language may be consciously molded to reflect a desired message or perspective via the observation of non-verbal interaction as well as through the process of training oneself.

The use of manipulation is not inherently evil.

To exert control over someone is to influence either their actions or their thoughts.

The use of conscious force is required for manipulation.

When you hear the word "manipulation," it's possible that the first thing that comes to your mind is something unpleasant. Take a rest and relax.

The use of manipulation is not inherently evil. Those who have nefarious purposes are.

Hypnotic Methods And Techniques

Opening a person's mind up to suggestion is the very first thing that has to be done in order to successfully hypnotise that person. The hypnosis specialist employs a wide variety of methods, and the final result might vary widely depending on the level of expertise possessed by the specialist as well as the receptivity of the individual being hypnotised.

One of the most prevalent forms of hypnosis is achieved via the practise of relaxation first. Have you ever heard an expert in hypnosis urge a person to make as much effort as they can to feel comfortable before beginning the hypnosis session? When this is done, the individual who is being hypnotised enters a state of relaxation in which their mind has a tendency to shut down on the local surroundings.

Unwinding may be accomplished by the following fundamental methods:

Get both your thoughts and your body to relax.

Calm yourself down

Mentally count from the highest number to the lowest.

Take command of what your body and mind are doing and how they are thinking.

Feel the tension melt away from your muscles as you relax.

Reduce the volume of your voice till it is hardly audible.

An experienced hypnotist will shake an individual's hand as part of the handshake approach for inducing hypnosis. Hypnosis experts, on the other hand, make use of this technique for another benefit, despite the fact that you could consider this to be a common approach for members of the public to meet or welcome one another.

They won't merely shake your hand; instead, they'll grip your wrist, twist it, or pull you towards them until you become unbalanced. It is just in that split second, when you are unstable, that the ideal chance presents itself for a professional in hypnosis to take control of your mind and direct your behaviour.

In hypnosis, eye suggestions are also capable of playing a crucial role. It is only normal for a person's eyes to stray to their surroundings or even catch a glimpse of something in the distance while they are conversing with another person. An expert in hypnosis will take this into consideration and, in a short amount of time, figure out what causes you to shift your eyes to the left, right, up, or down. They will then have access to how you think, feel, and react to particular things that are in your environment as a result of this.

One further strategy for inducing hypnosis in other people is to make mesmerising suggestions that aren't always clear. One kind of suggestion is one that is made by the hypnotist, and it involves something that the hypnotist wants the subject to perform. These suggestions are made after the consumer has already been put into a deeper stupor than they were before.

This is the point of time when people are most receptive to being influenced. The hypnotised person is not directly instructed to carry out a task; rather, the order is sent in the form of a cryptic suggestion. If you want someone to sit down, rather of telling them to "Sit down," you may say something like, "You should take a minute to relax in the chair over there."

One strategy that may help you enhance your hypnotic techniques is to record yourself when you are in a hypnotic state and then play back the recording. If you are able to hypnotise yourself completely, then you may be certain that you will also be able to hypnotise other people successfully. To get started, you should listen to several other recordings of hypnosis and figure out which techniques have worked best for you by listening to them.

After doing this, you'll be able to create your very own unique screenplay. Keep in mind that you should never hypnotise someone who has not given their permission to do so. Hypnosis helps the other person achieve a state of calm while also assisting in the process of persuading them to engage in behaviour that is good to themselves or others.

Practise is required to become proficient in each of these methodologies, just as it is with NLP. Do not allow yourself to get disheartened if, on your first attempt, you are unable to hypnotise another person completely. Make sure that you keep track of each and every hypnosis session that you undergo. What about it was successful the first time around but not as successful the subsequent times?

Keep in mind that you should not utilise any information obtained from another person when they were under the influence of hypnosis against them either. They are prone to falling into such a stupor at times that they enter a condition that is similar to dreaming. They may say something that isn't entirely true, much as someone who is on pain medicine after having their wisdom teeth out can say something that isn't entirely true.

In contrast to the practise of manipulation, the development of these talents is meant to also result in positive outcomes. After you have put in some practise, you could discover that it is simple for you to hypnotise other people, but the primary reason you do it shouldn't be for your personal benefit. You and the person you are entrancing stand to profit from the hard work you have put into acquiring the talent. You, as well as the person whose behaviour you can affect, may benefit from these potent approaches and the NLP recommendations in a way that is beneficial and empowering, regardless of how you decide to use them.

Be conscious of the fact that accepting the offer to hypnotise another person entails accepting some responsibilities as well. They are giving you access to a vulnerable part of their mind, which is something they most likely would not provide to anybody else. When you make an effort to convince another person, you sign yourself up to take responsibility for any unfavourable results that may occur as a direct consequence of your influence.

Even if you are utilising these hypnotic tactics, it will take some time before you are able to have a healthy, good impact on the other person. It is a tremendous luxury to possess long-lasting persuasion that will be to the advantage of all parties, and it is up to you to discover a constructive approach to make use of this capacity.

It is essential to be knowledgeable about your core human rights and the manner in which you should not be treated in order to devise a plan for escaping from people who attempt to control you.

You have the right to have respect shown to you at all times and to be respected yourself.

to articulate how you are feeling, your thoughts and beliefs, as well as the things you desire and need.

to choose your own priorities and objectives on your own.

to be able to reject something and not feel bad about it afterwards.

to receive the benefits of one's financial investment free of guilt or shame.

to have a viewpoint that is distinct from that of the other members of the group.

to advocate for one's own interests.

must look out for your own wellbeing.

to shield oneself against psychic, mental, and emotional damage in the event that you are threatened or injured by it.

And to make your own life a joyful experience from start to finish.

These particular rights allow you to establish crucial limits, which will be of use to you in the future when it comes to providing protection. It is important for us to keep in mind that there will always be individuals in this world who do not regard these rights or us as people, but rather consider us as objects that they may utilise to go to the next phase. Do not give other people the power to control your life or take control of you. You alone own the ability and authority to make decisions about your own life. You are the only one in command of it, as well, so it is entirely up to you.

Maintain a safe distance from people that you suspect are attempting to influence you or other people. Watch how they behave when they are put in new environments with new individuals and see how they react.

Avoid placing blame on yourself, despite the fact that it is a typical reaction to have when someone is attempting to reveal your flaws and exploit them for their own benefit, even if it is common to feel this way. You have to keep convincing yourself that you are not the issue, and that they are only attempting to coerce you into relinquishing your control over the situation. If this happens, you should inquire about some very fundamental matters, such as whether or not your partner treats you with respect. Are they willing to negotiate with me? Do I have positive feelings about who I am even if I am in a relationship? And as a last question, can you tell me whether or not this connection is mutually beneficial?

When Does Telling Lies Turn Into Deception?

When you give falsehoods any serious consideration, you'll see that they practically have a scale to them. You may be able to get out of going to a party by using a small white lie about not having a babysitter available, but that's not very high on the scale. But if you lie about not having a babysitter, but you really don't need one because you're lying about having a kid, then that's a pretty big whopper of a lie to tell. So where exactly do we draw the line?

Small white lies, often known as fibs, typically do not have significant repercussions. But bigger falsehoods, particularly those that get compounded by repetition or addition, lead to a cycle of lying that ultimately becomes damaging to oneself, others, or both. This cycle may begin with a simple white lie but can quickly spiral out of control. This cycle is probably the line that can be drawn between telling the truth and engaging in deceit.

Deception may manifest itself in a variety of ways, including but not limited to: lying about one's job or life experiences; lying about the condition of one's relationships; lying by omission; and even lying in such a way that the liar eventually begins to believe their own falsehoods. Why do individuals persist in employing falsehoods when they know full well that they may inflict significant psychological damage?

The Implications of Lies in Everyday Life

This goes back to the 'tend or defend' reaction that was discussed before. Let's go a little more into the reasons why individuals would tell falsehoods for the motives stated before. The phrase "defend oneself" appeared first on the list of possible explanations. The need to protect one's own interests is a strong force. If you are in a relationship that is abusive to you, you may find it necessary to lie about where you have been to avoid being verbally or physically assaulted. This may be the case even if the area in question is one that would be considered entirely safe in a healthy relationship. If the person who abuses you believes that you were in the supermarket rather than having coffee with a friend, then you have lied in order to protect yourself from more abuse.

The second justification was to protect the safety of other people. This may be quite similar to the situation described above; but, in this case, the liar may be a mother who is trying to shield her children from an authoritative person who is emotionally or physically abusive. Another possible situation is an older sibling assuming responsibility for their younger sibling's misdeeds while, in reality, the younger sibling was the one who produced the mess or damaged the precious item. When one person is in trouble for something else, friends or colleagues may tell lies to protect the other person from the consequences of their actions.

The care that one takes of oneself comes in at number two on the list of reasons why individuals tell lies. There are numerous selfish reasons to lie, and it is probably the most popular cause as well. There are also many other reasons to lie. People tell lies in order to satisfy their own wants and needs and to coerce others into giving them what they want. People tell lies because they want other people to like them, and as a result, they embellish their own successes and accomplishments in order to make themselves seem to have more than they really have. We learn about this when there is an instance of fraud involving a transcript or résumé.

People commonly make lies to cover up an uncomfortable circumstance or to avoid a difficult social contact. These lies are not spoken maliciously, but rather with the intention of covering up the humiliating situation or avoiding the awkward social engagement. It's possible that you're telling these falsehoods in order to cover up a mistake or get out of going to a party that you don't want to. Even though they are harmless fibs, you may get in trouble if your husband's obnoxious cousin finds out that you weren't really too sick to attend the wedding shower that was two hours away from where you said you were.

The last type of lies consists of those that individuals tell in order to take care of other people. In this context, "lying about liking someone's new haircut" or "lying about how good someone is at their job to help them get a good reference" are examples of dishonest behaviour that fall under this category. There is a general tendency for the falsehoods that we make in order to take care of other people to be of a good character; nevertheless, this does not imply that these particular lies will not be subject to the same adverse effects as other sorts of lying.

The use of NLP in medicine

The field of neuro-linguistic programming (NLP) treatments in medical and physical health is one that is relatively young. The interest in mind-body health, which is often referred to as integrative health or medicine, complementary medicine, or alternative medicine, has grown along with the growth of this field.

This argument is based on the idea that all mental states are tied to corresponding bodily ones. As a result, one should also consider the significance of one's internal representations and filters. For instance, if a person gets cancer, they think of themselves in the context of a cancer patient. This is a representation used inside the organisation. In addition to this, it is also connected in a very tight way to both their condition and their filters. When I asked a woman who had 16 tumours in her mouth about her belief that her mind was so strong that it made her ill, she said that she came to that conclusion on her own. Her meta-programs were those of a victim, which included avoiding motivation and self-sorting as a means of survival. I spoke with her as to whether or not she was certain that her mind really was so powerful. The yes response came from her very instantly and was accompanied by strong emotions. After that, I suggested that if her mind was so strong, she may consider letting it cure her body because it was so powerful. Suddenly, she gave me a look that suggested she was perplexed. I had just made the implication that she may be able to alter her meta-programs to empower herself and become more motivated. After a few months had passed, she gave me a call to ecstatically notify me that her cancer had gone into complete remission.

Additionally, I was able to eliminate my allergies with the application of NLP. A skilled hypnotherapist named Ann King, who works in the state of Texas, is in possession of an efficient NLP methodology for the removal of allergies. This method has been of assistance to hundreds of patients who have had ongoing allergy issues.

Although using NLP for health concerns is slightly more contentious than using it for other applications and requires extensive scientific confirmation, I find that its general notion is quite similar to some of the principles that I use in the ANNH and Neurology of Suggestion courses. This is true despite the fact that using NLP for health issues needs considerable scientific validation. Because they are founded on established scientific research, they provide a significant amount of legitimacy to the instances that are addressed by many of the NLP writers who are known for their original thinking.

4. The Arguments in Favour

Justifying your requests improves your chances of persuading the other person to carry out the desired act of kindness, despite the fact that you may not feel this to be true. In one of the experiments that was carried out by the researchers, a lady went to five different places and asked people, "Could you pick up the five pages of Xerox for me?" People did not answer to her request in a manner satisfactory to her sixty percent of the time. After that, the same test was carried out, but this time with the reason "because I have so much work here that I will not be able to arrive on time," and almost 94% of the respondents answered immediately to the request! When you need to submit a request in the future, be sure to include a justification for the cause!

5. Close Relationships

According to a number of studies, one of the most effective strategies for exerting influence on another individual is to strengthen the links between the parties involved. Making someone else happy in your company, or emotionally involving them, is the easiest method to exert influence on that person. This is because happiness is a powerful motivator. The formation of an emotional connection is something that researchers have found to be facilitated by participating in some kind of activity with the other person. It's possible that at first glance you'll think it's rather difficult, but in reality, it's not. For instance, you may discuss the songs you enjoy as well as share the music you listen to with other people. This will give them the impression that they are linked to you.

6. Pay Closer Attention

It is likely that you will be successful with this method if you are an extremely reserved and inwardly focused individual. Do not be concerned, though, if you are someone who is naturally more outgoing. According to a number of studies, persons who listen more intently in the job or at social events establish themselves in a position of influence over others around them. When confronted with a challenging circumstance, make an effort to maintain self-control and pay close attention to all the other person has to say. You may anticipate them asking you for your viewpoint on something. When a situation like this arises, the caller will focus their whole attention on you, making it much simpler to have a good chat with them. Using this strategy will boost your credibility and position you as the participant with the most significant perspective in any conversation.

7. Be Honest When You Speak

Did you know that even white lies might wind up being more damaging than helpful in the long run? Demonstrate to the individuals in your immediate environment that your life is not predicated on speaking falsehoods in order to make someone else happy, but rather that you have a character that is robust enough to speak the truth, even if it causes discomfort. If you are not dishonest, you will find that it is far more difficult to maintain control of the situation after you have lied about something and then slipped up.

The backstory is that your brain will naturally behave in the manner in which you have trained it to react.

A phobia is a learned aversion to a certain stimulus that occurs in everyday life.

Using this method, your brain will learn to respond differently when it sees something that it is afraid of.

After using this strategy, your brain will have two distinct courses of action available to it.

The first is the response of dread.

The second is to have a calm and collected demeanour.

The majority of the time, the brain wants to maintain its calm and relaxed state.

Criticising by name

You may even utilise it in situations when others are calling you derogatory or offensive names.

Maintain your composure and serenity despite the fact that you are being called a variety of derogatory names.

Reimagining of Oneself

When you alter the way you see yourself, your body will begin to adjust to reflect the new self-image.

Do you want to be thin and wealthy... Alter the way you see yourself, and you'll find that you begin to behave in a similar manner.

If three people tell you that you appear unwell, you will begin to question whether or not you really are sick.

When your attention is directed on finding indicators that you are ill, your mind will locate them.

Was the cough nothing more than a cough, or did it indicate the presence of cancer in the throat?

Is there a more productive use for that resource?

If, instead of searching for ominous indications, you were to seek for encouraging indicators...

After then, the cough was little more than a cough.

You should know by now that if you seek for anything, you will eventually find it.

If you seek for evidence of extraterrestrial life, you will find it everywhere.

How can you make it work to your advantage?

If being thinner is one of your goals, you should be on the lookout for indicators that you are successfully losing weight.

If you want to amass a lot of wealth, you should search for indications that you are making more money and spending less of it.

Accept The Responsibilities Associated

You are becoming pretty good at stopping yourself before blaming other people for the situation you're in, so now it's time to move on to the next phase in the process.

Accept responsibility for the things that are in your control. Analyse the current situation, determine the aspects of it over which you have power, and think about the ways in which you may exert influence for yourself. Do what you can with what you have, where you are, and how you feel. Simply ensure that these precautions prevent any other persons from intervening in any way in the situation.

As I made my way back to the United States from Canada in 2004, a post-psychotic emotional mess, I came to the realisation that meditation was going to be a significant component of my recovery.

The problem was that I was living in Glenorchy, which is a lonely community on the shore of a lake. There was only one route in and one road out of the area, and a yoga teacher lived there. In this backwater area, where there were no yoga instructors, I spent about a week becoming more irritable. As a result, I decided to study, looked for a yoga journal, and started a yoga practise at home. It has prevented me from dying. I was looking out for my own interests.

3. When you're attempting to put a halt to life, catch yourself in the act.

The activities of another victim that substantially impede one's capacity to fulfil the role of a master in life are acts of resistance to the way things now are. Whenever you find yourself thinking or saying anything along the lines of "I wish this wasn't going to happen... if only I hadn't done that... if only that... I hope I don't. ", stop and ask yourself why you are thinking or saying such things. You are, very simply, in conflict with reality. However, battling consumes an enormous quantity of energy for very little effect. Except for the discomfort.

Imagine you are standing in the middle of a fast-moving river and you are attempting to walk upstream while bracing yourself against the roar of the rapids. Consider what it would be like to be paddling downstream on the same rapid river while sitting in a kayak. It is not difficult at all.

When my parents split up, I was terribly upset, and by the time I was 12 years old, I looked like all Hell. This was shortly after the divorce. Every time we spent time with my dad, I would say that everything was shimmering and then proceed to shimmer myself. To give you the gist of it, I've taken every measure that a child my age can take to challenge the established order.

It has brought to a great deal of unneeded misery for both myself and the other members of my team. At the age of 12, I may be excused for not having complete control over my life. When we were 22, 32, or 42, we didn't have an excuse like that. It simply took place at this now. Just learn to accept it, buddy. And, certainly, this may at times require confronting challenging feelings;

thus, it is important that you be nice to yourself and that you surround yourself with others who are kind and sensitive.

The Method Of Integrating Individual Parts

There are aspects of who we are that nearly always find themselves at odds with one another. For instance, if you are aware that there is a blog that needs to be completed, there is a portion of you that acknowledges this reality and understands that you need to make time to sit down and do the task, but there is also a portion of you that does not want to complete the task because it wants you to watch your favourite movie that is about to be on television. The act of putting things off till later rears its ugly head at this point.

If you examine each of these components more deeply, you will see that they are all operating in concert to bring about inner tranquilly and contentment for you as an individual. Whether it is the part of you that wants to spend a little more time on Facebook or the part of you that wants to finish the blog, the primary goal of both of these aspects of you is to find inner calm and contentment. You may merge both of these aspects by using this common thread as a guide while you work towards accomplishing your goals and reaching your ambitions. You might get assistance with exactly this from the NLP approach known as "Parts Integration."

The Method for Quickly Overcoming Your Fears

You can also refer to this as the "Rewinding Technique," and it involves watching a video of the events that cause anxiety and rewinding it so that you can watch them in rapid-fire succession. This will enable you to observe the occurrences with a mind that is disassociated and detached, assisting you in understanding the difficulties that are there in an objective manner and finding solutions to those problems.

An human is able to reprocess and rewind the traumatic process with the use of the Fast Phobia Cure in NLP. This is accomplished while the individual remains in a safe and non-anxious zone. By going through this process, the person is able to rid both their body and their mind of the bad emotions associated with the traumatic occurrences. This is a fairly common method that is used by a large number of NLP coaches and trainers to assist their clients in overcoming a wide variety of ingrained fears and anxieties.

The method known as the "Circle of Excellence."

In order to accomplish what you want out of life and have a happy and fulfilling existence, it is just as essential to work on improving your strengths and cultivating positive emotions as it is to avoid or minimise the effects of negative emotions and concerns. Enhancing your good emotions and the qualities you already possess is the goal of the Circle of Excellence approach.

To cultivate an open mind and a diverse range of skills, you need to experience and feel positive emotions and sentiments. You can only acquire new abilities and recognise essential resources to advance along the career path of your choosing if you maintain a positive frame of mind. In order to construct your own circle of excellence, the core framework consists of the following steps:

The first thing you need to do is draw a circle on the ground, either mentally or, if at all feasible, literally. Check if the circumference of this circle allows you to fit within it.

The second step is to list all the positive aspects of who you are inside this circle. Make sure you include everything that comes to mind, including all the good deeds you've done, the sacrifices you've made, the goals you've accomplished, every other strength you possess, and every other source of optimism that is ingrained in you. Imagine these uplifting pictures as if they were contained inside a kaleidoscope that was made up of a variety of colours, moods, noises, and forms. Now, pose the following question to yourself. Do you want to have the same experiences that are taking on within the circle of excellence inside your own body and mind?

Step 3: At this point, physically enter the circle and focus on feeling energised by the good vibrations that emanate from your thoughts. Imagine a circle inside of you, and inside of that circle, see all of the colours and forms as well as the feelings and noises that you envisioned.

Proceed with this after you have this picture firmly established in your mind. Think about the coming week or month and think of all those occasions when you want this circle of excellence to be there for you. Imagine that this circle is placed under given circumstances. After that, take the meticulously crafted circle of perfection and put it somewhere secure, like your pocket or purse, so that you will always be able to utilise it again anytime you need it. The purpose of the NLP anchoring method is to help you get into a more optimistic frame of mind so that you can face impending obstacles with the proper mindset.

A Few Different Domains In Which Neuro-Linguistic Programming, Also Known As Nlp, Can Be Of Service To You

In addition to the benefits that were discussed above, the following are some more specific ways in which you may benefit from a Neuro-Linguistic Programming encounter with a trained NLP expert:

In the realm of gaming, NLP may be of assistance to you in removing obstacles and completing levels. It can also train your sensory system to produce groundbreaking designs that naturally "fire" during gameplay, so enabling you to achieve higher levels of peak performance.

In the context of interpersonal connections, Neuro-Linguistic Programming (NLP) can be of assistance in determining which modes of communication are most effective for oneself and the other party involved, as well as in learning how to communicate in ways that promote deeper comprehension and, consequently, feelings of compatibility or comparability between oneself and the other party. This unquestionably helps improve the quality of relationships you have with the people in your immediate environment.

Together, NLP and Timeline Therapy may help you cleanse and get rid of all the anger, difficulty, fear, pain, and guilt associated with the past. This is done by focusing on how you feel. The memories of such interactions will always be there; the only thing that will change is your connection to the bad emotions that were generated as a result of those experiences. It is obvious that as a result of this, you proceed with a stronger sense of calm.

In addition, Neuro-Linguistic Programming may be of assistance to you in removing any emotions of apprehension and anxieties that are limiting your life, as well as sensitivities, dyslexia, and other problems that conventional beliefs or medical practises would say are there to stay in your life. This can be the case even if these conditions have been there for a long time.

NLP helps you become more clear about your goals and ambitions, reveals the hidden blocks and limitations that are holding you back and teaches you how to overcome them, and then provides you with models of success and techniques that will speed up the rate at which you achieve your goals and dreams.

This list of benefits that may be enhanced via the use of Neuro-Linguistic Programming is most certainly not exhaustive, and there are a great many more ways in which you can profit from using NLP. If you are serious about creating the kind of life you image or foresee having and the existence of greater tranquilly, you should probably look into this topic a little bit further. You will have good karma if you live the extraordinary life you deserve.

One of the most helpful ways to think about mind control is as a system of influence that dramatically disrupts a person on a very fundamental level. The tactics that are employed in mind control have an effect on a person's identity, which includes his views, values, preferences, practises, behaviours, choices, and relationships, amongst other things. This results in the creation of a new pseudo-personality, also known as a pseudo-identity. You need to understand that mind control has the potential to be utilised for the victim's advantage. For example, it may be used to assist a drug addict in kicking their habit. On the other hand, in this specific instance, we are going to be focusing on the behaviours that are immoral and intrinsically problematic.

Philip Zimbardo, a psychologist, believes that mind control restricts either the communal or individual freedom of choice. He also argues that it is possible for anybody to become the target of mind control. Technically speaking, mind control is not an old and mysterious mystery that is only understood by a select few people; rather, it is a combination of words and grouped forces that are packed and presented in a manner that enables the victimizer to build dependence in followers. People that use mind control on others make decisions for their victims, but they trick their victims into thinking that they are autonomous and have the ability to make their own choices. The individual who is being controlled is often unaware of the methods and procedures that are being used, and he or she is also typically unaware of the changes that are taking place inside themselves.

You really must differentiate between these two things, since they are of vital importance. To begin, mind control is subtle, which means that the person who is subjected to it will rarely be aware of the changes taking place or the level of influence that is being exerted on him or her. It is important to be aware that this sneaky procedure may have disastrous results since it ensnares the victim and causes them pain. As a result of the subtlety of the influence, victims are led to believe that they are still in control of the choices pertaining to their lives, whereas in reality, other individuals are making those decisions for them. In addition, mental manipulation does not take place instantly; for this reason, the transformation is referred regarded as a process. It takes time - the length of time it takes depends on the tactics that were employed, the effects that were sought, the period of exposure, the capacity of the manipulator to influence, and personal characteristics. In today's world, there are certain manipulators who are so competent that they can accomplish their goals in a matter of hours. Even if there is no use of physical force in mind control, social and psychological factors and pressures are nevertheless put into play by those who are manipulating others.

Is it the same thing as brainwashing to influence someone's mind?

There are significant distinctions between mind control and brainwashing, despite the fact that both entail the manipulation of an individual's views in some way. To begin, mind control is always done in a covert manner, while brainwashing often involves some kind of physical coercion. During the process of brainwashing, the victim is made acutely aware of the fact that the victimizer is an adversary. For instance, in the situation of war captives, they are aware that their captor is an adversary, and they understand that their only chance of survival is to work together. In point of fact, the captors have the ability to employ physical force to get what they want. As a result, the inmates are forced to modify their beliefs in order to maintain their survival. On the other hand, after they have successfully escaped their captors, the effects of the brainwashing do not often last.

On the other side, mind control is more subtle, and the victimizer needs to be clever to guarantee that he/she is not recognised. The person doing mental control is usually a close person such as a teacher, a friend, or a spouse; thus, the victim will not suspect anything. In fact, it will not occur to them to take a defensive stand. To make matters worse, the victim might even be a willing participant because he believes the victimizer has good intentions. Furthermore, the victims will give information willingly, which the manipulator then uses to continue with mind control.

The fact that the majority of people who are subjected to mind control are not made aware of the goals of their manipulators makes the process of mind control a more perilous one than brainwashing. Because the effects of mind control will endure for longer, this comparison reveals that it may be possible for mind control to be more successful than other forms of abuse, including physical abuse, torture, and even drugs. Control does not include the use of physical pain, but it is far more successful than brainwashing. This is a crucial aspect to keep in mind.

Let's Get Started With The Anchoring

You now have a better understanding of the inner workings of your mind, as well as the definition of NLP and the anchoring method. In this chapter, I'm going to share with you some of my experiences, and I'm going to start with the easiest approach I've found to anchor emotions. The last chapter taught you an anchoring approach that is somewhat similar to this one, but this method is a little bit different.

When I host workshops and seminars, I always ask the attendees a single, straightforward question.

"How many of you remember listening to a wonderful presentation where you were impressed with the speaker?"

When I pose this topic to the participants and allow them some time to reflect on it, they take a seat, begin to think back to the presentations, and then raise their hands to respond to my inquiry. My following question is directed at those who have previously been exposed to an engaging presentation given by another individual, and it is phrased as follows: "What did you really like about the presenter?"

They will have to give extra thought to that specific presentation as a result of this query. They will remember the setting and the visuals that were in it, as well as the words that were said by the presenter and the thoughts that were going through their heads while they were watching the presentation.

They go back to that exact frame of mind that they were in on that day, which causes them to experience the same sentiments all over again as they attempt to recall the recollections and the specifics of the event in great detail.

I make a motion that is aimed at me as they start asking me questions and trying to get me to answer them. If somebody were to remark something like "The speaker was charismatic," for instance, I would casually tap the tip of my index finger on my chest in response. I would make the same motion if I found out that one of the participants had provided a good response. By acting in this manner, I am drawing all of the positive emotions closer to me. My action serves as my point of reference. Even if I don't make this move, the fact that the other participants are looking at me and talking to me will still lead those sentiments to become firmly rooted in me. The importance of direct communication and direct eye contact cannot be overstated in this context. These volunteers, whenever they thought of me in the future, would experience exactly the same sentiments all over again. From that point forward.

Then I proceed to ask them the second question that I have,

The Hypnotic State, Also Known As The Naturally Occurring Hypnotic State

Hypnosis refers to a state of mind in which a person's consciousness returns to its original, unaltered condition. Everyone, at some point in their life, is unknowingly subjected to hypnosis hundreds or perhaps thousands of times. You will enter a hypnotic state whenever you go to sleep and when you wake up again after you have been sleeping. With our assistance, you will be able to figure out how to make "naturally occurring tr states" work for your own personal development. There are also other occasions when we are in what is known as a naturally occurring tr state. If you have ever read a book, watched television, or participated in any other activity to the fullest extent, then you will eventually come to the conclusion that someone is saying something along the lines of "Hey! I'm addressing you directly!—you may call this a kind of hypnosis. If you have ever traveled from point A to point B and wondered what occurred in the little amount of time that elapsed ("A12"), then you have experienced a sort of hypnosis. When you engage in "automatic driving," your mind is temporarily diverted to other places while your body continues to move. In this scenario, driving has been transformed into an autonomous driving technology, a conditioned reaction that just needs your conscious and undivided attention, and everything may continue to operate as anticipated and "normally." Nevertheless, if there is any kind of emergency, you will instantly keep a watchful eye out for it and will take all precautions that are required. When you're driving and talking to other people, this might happen sometimes. You will drive pretty pleasantly while in this autopilot state until something arises that needs a precise choice... and the discussion has to end when you are completely actively thinking about driving.

How Neuro-Linguistic Programming (Nlp) Can Cure Ptsd More Efficiently Than Other Treatments Can.

A person who has experienced or seen a potentially life-threatening incident is more likely to acquire post-traumatic stress disorder, often known as PTSD. Both traditional and non-traditional approaches are used to treat post-traumatic stress disorder (PTSD), a condition that often has a wide range of repercussions.

Talk therapy, cognitive behaviour therapy, exposure therapy, and group therapy are all examples of traditional forms of treatment. Information processing, hypnosis, and neuro-linguistic programming (NLP) are all examples of alternative therapies for post-traumatic stress disorder (PTSD). The field of neurolinguistic programming (NLP) makes use of language in a unique way to reframe, redirect, and rearrange the way the brain codes experiences.

To put it another way, the primary focus of NLP is to modify emotional and mental behaviour patterns via the use of communication. The advantages of NLP greatly surpass those of any other treatment since it is such an efficient modality.

According to those who support the use of NLP.

As the number of people suffering from post-traumatic stress disorder (PTSD) continues to rise to concerning heights, there is an increasing need for a treatment that is both more efficient and effective. NLP has been proposed as a potentially effective therapy for people suffering from PTSD.

The structure of the traumatic experience, which proponents of NLP refer to as a superstimulus, is the primary emphasis of the NLP approach as opposed to the approach used by other therapies. This suggests that the effects of the trauma are even more severe than the incident that caused the trauma.

The fact that trauma may affect a person's perspective of reality and the way they see the world around them is one of the difficulties associated with learning to cope with it. Even if the traumatic event is so powerful that it causes a person to become desensitised, NLP is still able to overcome this hurdle.

NLP, which was established in the 1970s by Dr. John Grinder and Richard Bandler, has the potential to successfully alleviate the emotional suffering that is the direct outcome of traumatic experiences. NLP therapists serve more as facilitators and coaches than they do as subject matter experts. For the customer to feel like they own the project, they need to actively participate in the process.

Patient resistance, which is a typical impediment in other treatment techniques, is addressed and overcome in this way. NLP is a more participative kind of therapy than other methods, and the patient is actively involved in the progression of the intervention.

Neurolinguistic programming, or NLP, is comprised of neuro, linguistic, and programming components. By way of our senses, our nervous system takes in and analyses information about the happenings in our external world.

The relevance of neural representations is increased in spoken as well as nonverbal communication systems. Programming refers to an individual's ability to organise communication networks in order to accomplish a set of goals that they have set for themselves.

Through the use of the mind and language, NLP alters the way in which we perceive our external world, which in turn has an effect on the body and behaviour. The use of natural language processing breaks the connection between a person's memory of a traumatic experience and the information associated with it, such as their feelings at the time of the occurrence.

Patients suffering from post-traumatic stress disorder almost always exhibit the symptom of negative thinking reinforcement. NLP accomplishes its goals by separating representation methods from other aspects of human cognition and determining the contexts in which these strategies might be harmful. By doing so, NLP has the potential to change unhelpful beliefs into productive actions.

NLP makes use of the power of imagination as well as the power of the subconscious mind. on addition, NLP is effective because it places an emphasis on the here and now, determines the outcomes that are desired, and instructs the individual who is coping with PTSD on how to change their thought patterns.

The Psychology Of The Mentally Ill

In a Nutshell

In recent years, the field of psychology has worked towards the goal of elevating the human spirit through the use of several common concepts in the field, such as "social thinking," the various books written to teach the general public how to live a good existence through speaking in parachutes, the ten steps to anything, the mired in "how to," and a great number of other methods, and many more. A great deal is either the product of erroneous social cultures or the fashion du jour. Could living be as easy as picking up the right book and following the guidelines laid forth for you and I, and then everything in the world would be alright? This is a very unusual article in which we will investigate the "Evil" side of the human spirit. This is the half of mankind that considers detachment, destruction, and bad behaviour to be a normal and natural aspect of the human psyche, something that occurs in all of us from time to time. Why does civilization tolerate the darker aspects of itself? People who act in a manner that is in direct opposition to the cultural norms of society are referred to be "insane."

Let's have a look at how we may characterise the "other side" of social perception and behaviours in this article. We need a metric to be able to distinguish between behaviour that is considered normal and behaviour that is considered deviant. The first thing we are going to do is investigate social norms, which may be defined as what has been thought of as normal, day-to-day behaviour in any community, given a set of circumstances that test our view. For instance, in Western culture it is regarded both a criminal offence and an abhorrent behaviour in a peaceful society to physically strike a new person for the first time. On the other

hand, we back aggressive behaviour when the individual in question needs societal acceptability. This includes situations in which a warmonger, a police officer making an arrest of a violent criminal, and a local homeowner protecting his family from another person's serious assault fall under this category. Such contradictory anticipation is sure to cause confusion in a number of different ways. Whether it was a soldier committing war crimes such as genocide, a police officer using violence to harass a witness during the interrogation, or a citizen abusing the rights of another person in order to enhance his or her status, all of these actions constitute crimes against humanity.

Is there a reason to believe that the second test will be successful? What is not true, who will decide if such freedoms exist, do laws respect moral principles, and do they protect the weak from those who are affluent or those who are strong from those who are poor? Killing another person is considered immoral in the majority of world religions and civilizations. It is unequivocally immoral to take another person's life, and a society that upholds the moral law role that its legislators have assigned to the public needs to have the authority to punish those who engage in such conduct. This was a moral code of ethics for specific societies, such as the 10 ethical principles of Christianity and other comparable codes found in religions ranging from Buddhism to the Koran in the Islamic faith. Every civilised civilization has legal language and regulations that are considered to be the core of society because they convey the belief that there is a divine system of reward and punishment. Why do individuals readily break from moral, legal, and religious standards that, having accepted these norms, enable everyone to live in a peaceful society that is regulated by agreed-upon principles of behaviour that safeguard the person from danger, injury, and abuse?

The third aspect of behaviour is that it is not determined by laws or religious ideas; rather, it is determined by what the English language refers to as "managers" or "polite" in day-to-day conduct. The behaviours of a successful leader of a firm who knows how to behave in the company of people within a set of expectations that is viewed as the emblem of an established society are considered to be exemplary of that society. This may be seen at times in a table way protocol or in a guy who opens a woman's door and encourages her to recognise the duty of the male to protect and preserve her. Additionally, this can be seen in the actions of a man who opens a woman's door. In certain communities, the rights of women are not yet fully recognised, which casts doubt on the propriety of female behaviour and, as a result, diminishes the value of women. In spite of this, some behaviours are seen as a sign of a welfare community, regardless of whether they are traditional Englishness or the Japanese tea ceremony. These behaviours may be found in the upper echelons of society.

People frequently keep a wide variety of dysfunctions that also involve and control others, even in developed communities that have different measures taken, whether by legislation, morality, or reasonable social values. This is to the degree that those who perpetrate these behaviours are beyond the rules, moral codes, and behaviour of the rest of society. We all experience feelings of guilt from time to time when we realise that we have broken norms that are necessary for the functioning of a well-ordered society. However, there are other people who do not feel much in the face of abuse, ruin, and death towards another person as literally their right to survive without such laws and the freedom to lead an existence that is defined entirely by what they want, to possess or to murder. These people see the right to survive without such laws and the freedom to live an existence that is defined solely by what they desire as their right to survive.

CONCEALMENT OF INTENT

The act, whether large or tiny, poisonous or kind, of influencing followers to accept facts that is not real is what is meant by the term "deception." Deception may take many forms, but one of the most common is lying, which is defined as "the intentional communication of information that is known to be false." Any statement or behaviour that has the potential to convince another person of an untruth is capable of engaging in deception. Deception may take many forms, including but not limited to: giving proof for something that is not true, hinting that something is not true, concealing the truth, and lying. However, not every kind of deceit can be classified as dark psychology. Everyone will mislead people to some degree or another at some point in their lives. They might lead other people astray. After all, people experience feelings of inadequacy due to negative emotions such as embarrassment or even kindness. For instance, a number of studies have shown that many males are likely to exaggerate their claimed heights. This in no way indicates that they engage in negative forms of psychology. In addition, it is quite normal for individuals to lie to themselves about a variety of topics, including their level of happiness, their level of ambition, and their health.

Any time that deception is carried out with an apathetic or malicious purpose towards the victim, it is transformed into something more sinister. Understanding that the truth will not assist the deceiver's false purposes is an essential component of the dark kind of deception. The person who is perpetrating the deception will take the fact in question and either disregard it, suppress it, or modify it in order to favour a version of the events that more closely fits their aim. Those that engage in dark deceit do so with the intention of causing damage rather than providing assistance. They only care about furthering their own interests, even if it means hurting others in the process, and they have no remorse about this. Any size of deception may be perpetrated, from the personal to the global. Many people have the misconception that there must be widespread deceit for it to be required. However, dishonesty and trickery may be found in any area of the spectrum; thus, it is imperative that you be vigilant at all times in order to guarantee your own safety.

Many times, those who deal in dark deceit will rely on the assistance of the minor deceptions. They may begin with some of these little deceptions to try out the victim and create the necessary conditions for the victim to trust the larger falsehoods that the deceiver would utilise later on.

The victim's belief in their own capacities for reason and reasoning may also be undermined via the use of a smaller kind of deception. Imagine that the manipulator is able to trick the victim into believing something false about a less significant matter, and that the victim then begins to wonder what exactly is going on. In such a scenario, the victim can come to the conclusion that their suspicions were groundless and that they cannot put their faith in their own judgement. The vast majority of individuals will, almost immediately, come to the conclusion that the problem lies with their own judgement rather than even exploring the possibility that they are being misled by another party about an issue that on the surface seems to be relatively unimportant. Naturally, the evil person who deceives others is aware of the confidence that most people have, and they will make an effort to take advantage of it. A dark deceiver is capable of working with deceptions on a wide scale as well. Convincing another person that you are really someone else is one of the most effective forms of deceit that they may utilise. Not in terms of a single characteristic of one's personality or any other insignificant facet. A true liar is even capable of concealing their complete identities. They will conceal their identity, their date of birth, and everything else you ask them about. This is done in order to assist in furthering the aims or agenda of the manipulator in question. Even if the majority of individuals are truthful most of the time, there are situations in which even those who strive to be truthful engage in dishonesty. According to certain research, the average person lies many times every single day. Some of these falsehoods are significant ("I've never betrayed you!"), but the majority of the time, people use little white lies ("That suit looks perfectly fine") to get out of uncomfortable situations or to shield someone else's feelings.

What Exactly Is Meant By "Learning Capacity"?

Picture a balloon without air in front of you. All that is visible to us is that small elastic. Now imagine that air is inflating the balloon in your head. The airless balloon of the past has had significant growth and has undergone significant transformation. One thing that is probably very obvious is that the balloon will float higher the more air it contains inside of it. This bears some resemblance to the human brain and its correlation with an individual's overall functioning and performance. An individual becomes more proficient in his tasks the more knowledge he gains through education. In the language of science, this phenomenon is known as learning capacity.

A person has the natural ability to recognize and make use of the knowledge he has gained via the process of learning, claims Knowledge Works, a manual that teaches people how to use knowledge effectively in their lives. It also confirms that as a person's ability for learning grows, so does his or her method of learning. The more intriguing aspect of it is that humans have an endless capacity for learning, which may be explained by the neuroplasticity of the brain, which is the brain's natural tendency to rearrange itself. The phenomenon known as structural plasticity, a subtype of neuroplasticity, is the change in the brain's structure during the learning process, analogous to the balloon's physical appearance changing as air is pumped into it. Thus, as we continue to learn new things, our brain never stops working; rather, it only adapts as new knowledge and information are stored in it.

www.ingramcontent.com/pod-product-compliance
Lightning Source LLC
Chambersburg PA
CBHW052141110526
44591CB00012B/1808